D1709459

LAND FORMATION
The Shifting, Moving, Changing Earth™

THE CREATION OF
GLACIERS

Carol Hand

rosen publishing's
rosen
central®

New York

For Rowan—you make me proud

Published in 2010 by The Rosen Publishing Group, Inc.
29 East 21st Street, New York, NY 10010

Copyright © 2010 by The Rosen Publishing Group, Inc.

First Edition

Library of Congress Cataloging-in-Publication Data

Hand, Carol.
The creation of glaciers / Carol Hand.—1st ed.
    p. cm.—(Land formation: the shifting, moving, changing earth)
Includes bibliographical references and index.
ISBN-13: 978-1-4358-5298-3 (library binding)
ISBN-13: 978-1-4358-5594-6 (pbk)
ISBN-13: 978-1-4358-5595-3 (6-pack)
1. Glaciers—Juvenile literature. I. Title.
GB2403.8.H36 2010
551.31'2—dc22

2008054737

Manufactured in Malaysia

On the cover: The Perito Moreno Glacier in Patagonia, Argentina, has walls that tower more than 200 feet, or around 40 meters, and is a popular destination for tourists.

CONTENTS

Introduction...**4**

Chapter 1

The World of Ice...**6**

Chapter 2

Rivers of Ice...**13**

Chapter 3

Glaciers as Sculptors...**22**

Chapter 4

Frozen in Time...**32**

Chapter 5

Remnants of an Ice Age...**39**

Chapter 6

Glaciers Today and Tomorrow...**45**

Glossary...**54**

For More Information...**56**

For Further Reading...**58**

Bibliography...**59**

Index...**62**

INTRODUCTION

Imagine an astronaut looking down on the earth from space. There, beneath the wisps of white, swirling clouds is a gleaming marble—deep blue oceans, patches of green and brown land, both poles capped with smooth white sheets of ice. From space, this blue marble seems peaceful—a safe, comfortable place to live.

And that description is certainly true of many places on the earth. But no polar explorer would describe the icy landscapes at the North and South Poles as "safe" or "comfortable." The ice is not smooth at all. Miles of it are ridged and grooved, as though a giant comb has ripped through it. More miles are covered with jagged spears and chunks of ice, and in some places, deep cracks open up, big enough to swallow entire vehicles. At the edges of polar ice fields, huge cliffs drop straight down to meet the ocean.

Few ever experience this frozen environment in person. But people in the northern United States or Canada can see the work of past glaciers all around. In this book, we will explore the history and glacial processes that have created landforms ranging from the Great Lakes to Yosemite Valley.

Curving moraines of glacial till wind their way down Switzerland's Aletsch Glacier. Aletsch is the largest glacier in the European Alps.

THE WORLD OF ICE

Glaciers are made of ice, and ice is made of the same fresh-water that comes from the tap. The earth will never run out of water. The same water is recycled over and over as it continuously circulates through air, soil, water bodies, and living organisms. This circulation is called the hydrologic, or water, cycle. But the water cycling around the earth is only a tiny part of the planet's freshwater.

The Earth's Cryosphere

More than 75 percent of the earth's freshwater is trapped as ice. This frozen water—composed of sea ice and glaciers—is called the cryosphere.

Sea ice, in the form of icebergs, is found only at very high latitudes, in the polar oceans at the North and South Poles. Portions of the cryosphere that form on land are glaciers. Glaciers are found at the poles and at very high altitudes, such as the tops of mountains. If peaks are high enough and cold enough, glaciers can even exist in the hot tropics.

Today, glaciers cover only about 10 percent of the earth's surface. During the last ice age, about twenty thousand years ago, more than 30 percent of the earth's surface was

These Gentoo penguins are at home on an iceberg in Antarctica's Gerlache Passage. Few other animals are so well adapted for polar life.

covered with ice. Glaciers extended from coast to coast as far south as the central United States. If that much ice existed today, the cities of New York and Chicago would be buried under ice sheets several thousand feet thick.

What Is a Glacier?

A glacier is a very thick sheet of ice that has formed on land over hundreds or thousands of years. Glaciers form when snow builds up, forms crystals, and compresses. For snow to build up and form a glacier, more snow must fall than melt.

HAZARDS ON ICE

Glacier travelers should have basic mountaineering skills before crossing a glacier. Here are a few hazards for which every glacier explorer must be prepared:

CREVASSE! Crevasses are long, deep gaps in snowfields, and they are the major hazard on any glacier. Crevasses on Alaskan glaciers may be up to 60 feet (20 meters) across and 165 feet (50 m) deep. Crevasses are particularly dangerous just after a snowfall, when new snow may hide them.

MOAT! A glacier melts from the edges, leaving a gap between the glacier and the mountain walls enclosing it. The gap fills with meltwater, forming a moat. Moats can be even deeper and more dangerous than crevasses.

AVALANCHE! An avalanche can consist of loose snow or chunks of ice that plummet downhill, crushing and burying everything in their path. This often happens when a slab of overhanging ice breaks off because it becomes too heavy or is weakened by melting.

As an avalanche of snow and ice hurtles down a mountainside, it carries soil, rock, and other debris with it.

THE WORLD OF ICE

Glaciers thrive in regions that have extreme climates. Almost 99 percent of the earth's land-based ice is found above 60° north and below 60° south latitudes, surrounding the North and South Poles. At the poles, summers are so short and cool that they almost don't exist. And winters are so long and cold that snow can accumulate for thousands or even millions of years without melting! Huge glaciers called ice sheets, or continental glaciers, form on large, flat land areas. Only two ice sheets exist today: the Greenland Ice Sheet in the Northern Hemisphere and the Antarctic Ice Sheet in the Southern Hemisphere. Smaller, flat glaciers very similar to ice sheets form on high plateaus or mountaintops in polar regions. These glaciers are called ice caps or ice fields.

Ice sheets and some ice caps extend outward to an ocean or sea. Sometimes, huge slabs of glacial ice flow completely off the land and extend out over the ocean, forming ice shelves. When pieces of ice shelves break off, or calve, the ice chunks fall into the ocean and form icebergs. Most ice shelves are in Antarctica. The largest is the Ross Ice Shelf, which is as big as the country of France.

Mountain, or alpine, glaciers form near the tops of the world's tallest mountains. These high altitudes also have extreme climates. In fact, they are very similar to polar climates. But there are no flat plains where ice sheets or ice caps can form, so mountain glaciers are much smaller. Many of them are tucked into the valleys between mountain peaks. Sometimes, tongues of ice from mountain glaciers or ice caps extend downward below the snowline, even into temperate rain forests.

Birth of a Glacier

A glacier begins in a high, cold region of the earth. Snow falls, and because little melting occurs, it builds up. Each new layer pushes down on the layers below. As the snow cover becomes

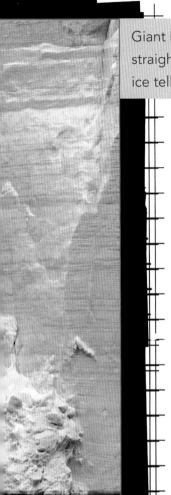

Giant ice cliffs at the edge of the West Antarctic Ice Sheet drop straight down to the Weddell Sea. Different colored bands of ice tell the glacier's year-by-year history.

thicker, it presses harder on the deeper layers. The deepest layers compress to form ice, and a glacier is born.

How long it takes snow under pressure to become ice depends mostly on temperature and the amount of snowfall. For example, at both poles, almost no precipitation falls in some areas. These regions are called polar deserts because less than 10 inches (about 250 millimeters) of precipitation fall in a year. Antarctica gets less than 2 inches (5.08 centimeters) per year. So ice and snow accumulate very slowly. The oldest ice in Greenland is probably about 110,000 years old. Some ice in Antarctica may be forty million years old. At both poles, the change from snow to ice may take hundreds of years.

In temperate mountain glaciers, meltwater helps change snow into ice. Melting can cause glaciers to form very rapidly—in only five to ten years, instead of hundreds of years. As meltwater trickles through the top layers of snow, the snowflakes begin to break apart and compress. Lower layers compress more. The compression changes flat, star-shaped snowflakes into rounded grains, much like grains of sugar. The upper layers of snow grains have air spaces between them, but as the deeper snow compresses, it pushes out the air. This stage halfway between snow and ice is called firn, which means "old snow."

In temperate mountains, firn forms from snow that is one to two years old. Firn is about ten times denser than snow and about half as dense as water.

After five to ten years, as more snow is deposited on top, the firn compresses further to form true glacier ice. Ice takes the form of crystals, which can become very large. If you look at an ice cliff, you can see layers of different kinds of snow and ice. These layers show individual years of snow accumulation, much as tree rings show annual growth of a tree. The youngest layers of snow are at the top of the cliff. Below this are layers of firn having fewer and fewer air spaces as you go down. Finally, nearest the bottom are thick layers of dense, crystalline ice—the oldest part of the glacier.

No two glaciers are exactly alike. Individual glaciers vary according to location. A mountain glacier near the coast receives much more precipitation than an inland glacier. This determines whether the ice is spongy or solid and how fast it compresses. Also, glaciers change constantly as they react to weather and climate. If there is heavy snowfall and little melting during the year, the glacier advances. If the weather is warm, it retreats. And glaciers change as they move downhill due to gravity. Huge chunks of ice may break off the edges of glaciers due to melting or internal stresses. In mountain glaciers, this causes an avalanche. At the edge of an ice sheet, the ice falls into the ocean and forms a new iceberg.

CHAPTER 2

RIVERS OF ICE

Glaciers move and change in two ways. First, they advance or retreat from year to year. A glacier advances when snow falls and retreats when snow melts, so it changes in size. Second, glaciers move downhill in response to gravity and other forces. Downhill movement is like river flow, but much slower.

Glacial Advance and Retreat

We can tell if a glacier is advancing or retreating by looking at its mass balance, which is like the glacier's budget. Just as a family saves or spends a certain amount of money, a glacier saves or spends snow and ice. Sometimes, a glacier adds more snow than it melts. This glacier has a positive mass balance and is growing. At other times, the glacier is losing more snow or ice than it is adding. This glacier has a negative mass balance and is getting smaller. So mass balance is the relationship between addition and loss of snow or ice. For a glacier to stay the same size, these values must be equal. That is, the glacier must balance its budget of snow and ice.

Scientists can measure the gain or loss of small mountain glaciers directly. They insert measuring rods into the snow at

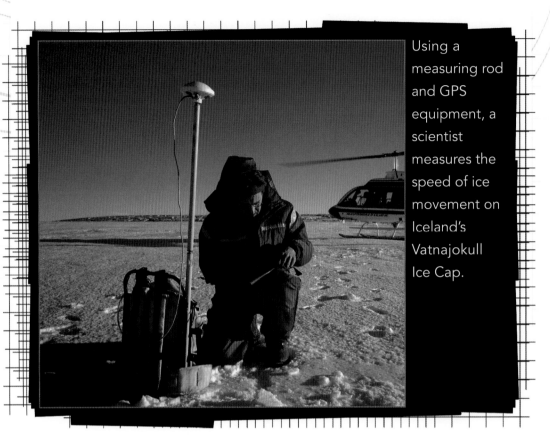

Using a measuring rod and GPS equipment, a scientist measures the speed of ice movement on Iceland's Vatnajokull Ice Cap.

both the top and bottom of the glaciers. They measure the change in snow depth or the retreat of snow from the rods at the beginning and end of the melting season. They must do this every year for decades to get useful records. Ice sheets are far too large to measure this way. Instead, scientists use satellite photos, radar, and lasers to compare the changes in ice sheets from year to year.

A mountain glacier has definite zones where snow is added or lost. Snow is added at the top of the glacier. Here, the temperature is colder, more snow falls, and less snow melts or evaporates.

Snow is lost downhill, toward the bottom of the glacier. Here, the glacier loses more snow than it gains. The region between these two zones, where gain and loss of snow are exactly balanced, is called the firn line.

In areas where snow is being added, weight and pressure increase. The deepest snow is compressed into ice. Increased pressure and gravity combine to push this ice downhill. Most downhill ice is lost by melting or evaporation. But sometimes glaciers calve, just as ice shelves form icebergs. At the edges of mountain glaciers where steep drop-offs occur, calving causes avalanches. This leaves massive fields of tumbled ice chunks at the glacier's base. These fields are called icefalls, and they are treacherous to cross.

The smaller the glacier, the faster it changes. Small mountain glaciers grow during cold, snowy years and shrink during warmer, drier ones. But large glaciers in the same area may show little change for fifty years or more. The earth's climate has become gradually warmer since the late 1800s and is warming even faster now. As a result, most mountain glaciers have become much smaller. Some may even disappear in the next ten to twenty years.

Ice sheets add ice in their centers and lose it at the edges. They are immense compared to mountain glaciers, so they change much more slowly. The Antarctic Ice Sheet covers an area larger than the United States and Mexico combined, and in its deepest part, the ice is more than 2.5 miles (4 kilometers) thick. Because of its huge size and extremely low precipitation, the mass balance of the Antarctic Ice Sheet has been very stable until

recently. But, as we will see later, rising global temperatures may now be affecting it, too.

The Greenland Ice Sheet covers only one-seventh as much land area as the Antarctic Ice Sheet. Because it is so much

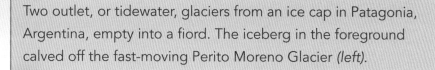

Two outlet, or tidewater, glaciers from an ice cap in Patagonia, Argentina, empty into a fiord. The iceberg in the foreground calved off the fast-moving Perito Moreno Glacier *(left)*.

smaller, it changes more quickly. The continents of Europe and North America and the Arctic Ocean all affect its climate. It accumulates twice as much snow as Antarctica. Also, southern Greenland has a short summer season during which meltwater flows off the ice sheet into the ocean. In the first decade of the 2000s, satellite photos show it is becoming noticeably smaller.

Downhill Glacial Movement

Glaciers are never still. A mass of snow and ice only becomes a glacier when it is large enough to flow. For a mountain glacier, this means it is at least 65 feet (20 meters) thick. Like a flowing river, it moves downhill with gravity, but much more slowly. Fast-moving glaciers can move 10 feet (3 m) or more per day. Others move so slowly that trees have time to grow on them. The average mountain glacier moves less than 3.25 feet (1 m) per year. Besides gravity, three other processes help glaciers

GLACIER SURGES

Most people think glaciers always move slowly. But sometimes glaciers surge, or suddenly speed up without warning after creeping forward very slowly for decades. Pressure builds up in the ice, and complex crevasses break open at the glacier surface. A surging glacier can flow several hundred times faster than normal and can push forward miles, instead of just a few inches.

Over a period of seventeen months starting in 1993, Alaska's Bering Glacier surged 5.6 miles (9 km) downhill and dumped huge amounts of ice and till into Vitus Lake, at its base. It buried two small islands and several large colonies of nesting geese and waterfowl.

flow downhill: plastic deformation, basal sliding, and movement over till.

Plastic Deformation

If something is "plastic," it can be molded into a different shape, just as a handful of Silly Putty squishes when you squeeze it. How much the shape changes depends on the amount of pressure exerted—that is, how hard it is squeezed. The new shape depends on where the pressure is exerted. If you squeeze the putty harder with your thumb and forefinger, the front part becomes longer and thinner and the back becomes thicker. Even though the putty seems solid, pressure changes its shape. This is plastic deformation.

In glaciers, plastic deformation is also called plastic flow, or creep. Creep happens only in ice below about 100 to 165 feet (30 to 50 m) deep, depending on the glacier. This narrow region below which creep begins is called the zone of fracture. Above this region, ice is under less pressure. It is brittle and it fractures, just as a pane of glass would crack if you stepped on it. When ice fractures, it forms a crevasse. Below the zone of fracture, plastic flow closes the crevasse. This is why crevasses are never hundreds of feet deep. In this deep region, where pressure is greatest, ice moves forward by plastic flow. It is like a giant hand is closing around it and pushing it forward. The brittle ice above the zone of fracture is just carried along for the ride.

Basal Sliding

"Basal" refers to the base of the glacier. In basal sliding, ice slips and slides along a thin layer of meltwater between the ice and the bedrock beneath it. The moving ice melts due to friction or heat from inside the earth. The meltwater lubricates the ice above and helps it flow across the base. As the ice slides, it creates more friction. This creates more heat, which melts more ice, making the glacier slide more easily. The more meltwater, the faster the glacier can move. So glaciers move faster in summer than in winter.

Movement Over Till

Movement over till occurs when a glacier flows over sediment, rather than bedrock. This sediment, called glacial till, consists of bits of rock and soil ranging in size from clay particles to large boulders. It mixes with meltwater to form a thick slush. A moving

A glacier moves downhill into a fiord in Glacier Bay, Alaska. The dark line down the center is a medial moraine (see chapter 3).

glacier plows easily through glacial till, deforming the sediments as it passes. It carries along much of the till and deposits it downhill.

We can follow the movement of a temperate glacier by observing patterns in the ice itself. As ice accumulates, it forms a new layer each year. As the ice moves downhill, it moves faster in the center than at the sides. This results in a regular series of curves, called ogives (OH-jives), that show the direction of ice flow.

Even huge ice sheets flow very slowly downhill toward the coast. Valleys in the center of the ice sheet form drainage basins or ice streams, where ice flows much faster than in the surrounding ice walls. Sometimes, as ice streams reach the coast, they continue to flow outward over the ocean without melting. This is how ice shelves are formed.

GLACIERS AS SCULPTORS

Glaciers are nature's artists. They sculpt the landscape by two processes: erosion and deposition. Erosion is like a sofa being moved across a wood floor. It wears away the rock or soil beneath a glacier and sculpts mountain peaks and deep lakes. Glaciers are also called nature's conveyor belts because they carry eroded material along and deposit it in new locations. This deposition is similar to the piles of wood shavings left behind by the moving sofa.

Glacial Erosion

Glacial erosion works in two ways: plucking and abrasion. Plucking occurs when meltwater seeps into cracks within rock, refreezes, and expands. This changes the pressure on the rock and causes it to break. Plucked rocks and pebbles, even boulders, become part of the glacier and are pushed along with it. As the glacier moves, the plucked rocks grind against the bedrock underneath, leaving parallel scratches, or striations. These striations are snapshots of the glacier's movement. You can see the southward movement of glaciers from the last ice age in the striations left in the exposed bedrock of New York City's Central Park.

A "boulderer" climbs Rat Rock (also called Umpire Rock) in New York City's Central Park. Striations on glacial rocks like this trace the history of the last ice age.

Avalanches and rockslides are probably the most spectacular forms of glacial erosion. They occur when thawing and refreezing on a steep mountainside cause huge chunks of the mountain to break off and crash to its base. In 1991, the summit of Mount Cook, New Zealand's highest mountain, collapsed. The mountain is now more than three stories, or 30 feet (9.14 m), shorter.

Glacial Erosion in Mountains

Glacial erosion has created some of our most breathtaking mountain scenery. These mountains often have sharp peaks,

steep sides, or deep troughs. Erosion in mountainous regions also produces other unique landforms.

U-shaped valleys are formed by glacial erosion. A river flowing through a valley produces a V-shaped channel. During an

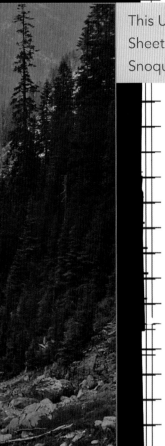

This U-shaped valley was carved out by the Cordilleran Ice Sheet more than 10,000 years ago. It is in the Mount Baker-Snoqualmie National Forest in Washington State.

ice age, a glacier forms and completely fills the riverbed with ice. As the ice slowly flows downstream, it cuts the valley deeper and wider until it eventually becomes U-shaped. It is now called a glacial trough. Smaller rivers that once emptied directly into the main river are left hanging above the valley floor, like a high diving board over a swimming pool. These are called hanging valleys. Water flows over their edges into the deeper valley below, producing beautiful waterfalls. In California's Yosemite National Park, Yosemite Valley is a glacial trough with many hanging waterfalls flowing into it.

A cirque (rhymes with "jerk") forms when glacial ice accumulates in a small depression at the head of a valley. The ice deepens and widens the depression, forming a bowl with three steep sides and an open side facing down the valley. After the glacier melts, the bowl, or cirque, fills with water. This forms a glacial lake, or tarn. The brilliant turquoise Lake Louise, in Canada's Banff National Park, is a tarn.

As a cirque erodes, it produces an arête (uh-RET), or a ridge having a very sharp, pointed peak and steep sides. A single peak, called a horn, develops when several eroding cirques surround a single mountain. The Matterhorn, in the Swiss Alps, is probably the most famous horn.

A fiord (pronounced "fee-ORD" and also spelled "fjord") is sometimes called a drowned river valley. Fiords are ocean inlets that were once glacial troughs. They occur where mountain ranges come down to the edge of the ocean. When ice from the last ice age melted, sea levels rose and these glacial troughs were submerged. Norway is famous for its fiords.

Glacial Deposition

The products of erosion, or glacial till, range in size from clay and sand particles to huge boulders. Glacial till of all sizes is carried along with the ice, and eventually, as the ice melts, till is deposited far downstream. Deposition has covered the bedrock of our country's northern plains with hundreds of feet of glacial till. This material has given us both the rich farmlands of the Midwest and mineral deposits—from gravel to diamonds—for the mining industry.

Moraines are probably the largest, most obvious landforms made by glacial deposition. A moraine is a long ridge of till pushed along and deposited by an advancing glacier when it begins to melt.

A curved ridge called a terminal moraine forms at the very tip, or snout, of a valley glacier or ice sheet. While ice is melting at

Terminal and lateral moraines, or ridges of glacial till, are evidence of glacial sculpting around Convict Lake in California's Sierra Nevada Mountains.

the glacier's snout, the ice behind it continues to push forward like a bulldozer, piling the till in front of it. Moraines formed from ice sheets can extend for hundreds of miles. A long section of the East Coast of the United States—including Long Island, Nantucket, and Cape Cod—was formed when two terminal moraines were deposited fourteen thousand and twenty thousand years ago during the last ice age. At lower elevations, lateral moraines form along the sides of a valley glacier. Medial moraines form when two valley glaciers curve toward each other, meet in the middle, and flow downhill together.

Sometimes, even after till is deposited, the glacier continues to advance over it. Because till is soft and easily molded, the flowing glacier sculpts collections of small, streamlined hills. They have a gently sloping side showing the direction of ice movement and are steep on the other side. These hills, called drumlins, are often found in large groups called drumlin fields. Drumlins are usually no more than 50 to 200 feet (15,24 to 61 m) high. They are common in New England and the northern British Isles.

Finally, glacial deposition also forms eskers, or curving ridges of sand and gravel. Eskers form when streams of water flow in tunnels under the glacial ice. They can wind snake-like across the landscape for hundreds of miles. In Finland, roads have been built on flat-topped eskers. In the United States, many eskers have been mined for sand and gravel.

Carving Glacial Lakes

Hundreds of thousands of small lakes in Canada and the United States today were formed by glaciers. Minnesota, for example,

GLACIAL ERRATICS

"Erratic" means unexpected or out of place. Erratics are very large pieces of glacial till that were carried by glaciers and deposited many miles from their origin.

They stand out because of their size and because they are made of different types of rock than the bedrock on which they sit. This difference gave geologists their first clue that glacier movement might have deposited erratics.

Pilot Rock in Iowa is one of a long string of similar erratics called a boulder train. Rocks in this boulder train contain a pink mineral called Sioux quartzite. Boulders extend from South Dakota through southwest Minnesota and into northwestern Iowa. Every pink rock along the way, including Pilot Rock, marks the path of the glacier that deposited it.

Not all erratics are part of boulder trains. Some stand alone. The largest known erratic, in Alberta, Canada, is simply called Big Rock. It weighs 16,500 tons—as much as 412 fully loaded eighteen-wheelers!

pays tribute to its glacial past by calling itself "The Land of 10,000 Lakes." Moraines, eskers, and other glacial deposits were dropped into this landscape. Some of them formed dams, and when the ice melted, the areas behind the dams filled to become lakes.

Very small lakes or ponds, called kettles, often formed in front of moraines. As meltwater flowed through channels in the moraines, it carried some of the till and spread it over the flat areas beyond, forming outwash plains. Sometimes, large chunks

Banff National Park in Alberta, Canada, is home to beautiful Lake Louise. Meltwater from the glaciers above carries rock flour that gives the lake its brilliant turquoise water.

of ice were deposited with the till. When the ice melted, it left depressions that formed kettles. Walden Pond, near Concord, Massachusetts, is a famous kettle.

The Great Lakes are one of the most striking examples of glacier action. Between about seventy thousand and fifteen thousand years ago, an ice sheet 2 miles (about 3.22 km) thick—the Wisconsin Glacier—covered the region that is now Canada and the northern United States. This was the last of four glaciers that scoured our continent during the most recent ice age. The grinding movement of these glaciers scooped out five gigantic basins. When the Wisconsin Glacier finally began to melt, about fifteen thousand years ago, its meltwater filled these five basins. Today, we call them the Great Lakes.

CHAPTER 4

FROZEN IN TIME

We expect climate to be fairly predictable. The Midwest has four seasons a year. The South has warm weather with summer hurricanes. Southern California is warm and sunny year-round. But the earth's climate was not always like this. It has been a series of repeating cycles, with long warm periods followed by shorter periods of icy cold. During these cold periods, or ice ages, glaciers pushed far south from the North Pole—sometimes almost to the equator. Ice ages are one of science's greatest puzzles. The time periods involved are very, very long, and each new ice age overwrites most of the evidence of earlier ones.

Since the 1700s, people have looked for clues to the earth's history. They have uncovered many glacial features: sculpted mountains, lake basins, moraines, and erratic boulders. But it took time to figure out that vanished ice sheets had made these landforms. For many years, people thought they were caused by flowing water.

As scientists tried to explain how glaciers could have changed the landscape, they also developed methods to determine the extent of ice coverage, the dates of ice ages, and even some of their possible causes. We are still a long

Italian hikers enjoy the view across the Rutor Glacier from the top of a glacial erratic.

way from understanding what starts and ends an ice age, but this problem is important to all of us. Our current climate is changing rapidly, and we must understand what caused past climate cycles if we are to prepare for the coming changes.

Documenting Ice Ages

People tend to measure time in terms of the human lifespan. Most people live no more than one hundred years, so things that happened much further back in history often don't seem very important. But geological time is measured in chunks of

The boatswain on this Canadian Coast Guard icebreaker lowers a box corer to collect ocean-floor sediment. Sediment cores provide scientists with valuable information about past climate change.

thousands or millions of years. Ice ages extend far back into the earth's history, long before humans even existed. Because we were not even here for most of this story, we must find indirect evidence of ancient climates.

We do know that a major cause of changes in the earth's climate—including ice ages—is the amount of sunlight the earth receives. The distance between the earth and the sun varies because the earth's orbit is not exactly circular. As this distance changes, so does the amount of sunlight we receive. Sunlight also varies with the tilt of the earth's axis toward or away from the sun. The amount of tilt varies by several degrees over a

41,000-year cycle. But these changes are not the only factors causing ice ages.

The amounts of carbon dioxide and other greenhouse gases present in the atmosphere are also important. Greenhouse gases trap the sun's heat and move it through the atmosphere. They keep our planet warm enough to support life. If their levels drop, temperatures become colder. If they increase, temperatures become hotter. So levels of greenhouse gases also give us clues to early climates.

Levels of oxygen tell a climate story, too. Ocean sediments are like books we can read to reveal the mysteries of ancient climates. Sediments build up in layers, forming a continuous record of changes. The top layer of a core is the most recent, and the bottom layer is the oldest. Sediments include shells, which contain oxygen from seawater. By measuring amounts of two different types of oxygen in the sediment, scientists can determine the temperature of the seawater when the shells were made. So they drill sediment cores in the ocean floor and measure oxygen levels from top to bottom to develop a historical record of water temperatures. The deepest core obtained so far was drilled off the coast of Antarctica. It was more than a mile (1.6 km) long and its deepest sediments were thirty-four million years old.

We can also read ice cores from existing glaciers to learn about ancient climates. Ice cores contain pockets of gases that are tiny time capsules. By reading the amounts of carbon dioxide in ice cores from top to bottom, scientists can piece together a picture of how the earth's atmospheric temperature changed. The higher the level of carbon dioxide at a given level, the higher the temperature was then. Ice cores give us a detailed, year-by-year

GLACIALS AND INTERGLACIALS

Ice ages have periods of extreme cold called glacials. During glacials, the ice pushes forward and glaciers reach their largest size. Between glacials are shorter periods called interglacials. Then, temperatures warm and most or all of the ice melts. During these times, sea levels around the world rise as melted ice from continental ice sheets flows into the oceans.

In the last eight hundred thousand years, the earth has experienced eight glacial and interglacial cycles, each about one hundred thousand years long. During each cycle, ice builds up gradually, so the glacial period lasts a long time. During the interglacial period, the ice melts very quickly and sea levels rise. The most recent ice age peaked about twenty thousand years ago. At that time, ice covered about 30 percent of the earth's surface.

Because major ice melting began about ten thousand years ago, we are currently in the middle of an interglacial. In another ten thousand years, unless human activities continue to heat the planet, ice will begin to form and ice sheets will roll down from the North Pole, covering many northern cities.

account of the most recent climate changes. The deepest ice core from Antarctica stretches back almost 750,000 years.

The Distant Past

During most of the earth's 4.54-billion-year history, average temperatures have been much warmer than they are now. But ice ages have occurred over and over, too. The further back in history an ice age happened, the less we know about it, but traces remain. We can determine the ages of rocks with glacial markings. During every ice age, much of the life on the planet goes extinct. After the ice age ends, the remaining species evolve very rapidly and spread out to fill the many empty habitats. These changes are recorded—later ones better than very early ones—in the earth's fossil record.

We know of two extremely early ice ages: the first about 2.9 to 3 billion years ago and the second about 2 to 2.5 billion years ago. During both of these ice ages, all life on the earth was single-celled and very simple. Many of these primitive species probably died off, and new species evolved.

After the second ice age, there was no evidence of cooling for as much as 1.4 billion years, or 30 percent of the earth's history. During this time, simple invertebrates, including snail-like creatures, evolved to fill the warm oceans. Then, starting about one billion years ago, we have records of at least six definite glacial periods.

One of these glacial periods, between about 550 and 850 million years ago, was so extreme that it may have caused the earth to ice over completely. On this "Snowball Earth," even the oceans may have frozen and average temperatures matched those on Mars today. No one is sure what triggered this icy plunge in temperature. But, whatever the trigger, it must have caused most ocean life to become extinct.

"Our" Ice Age

We are now experiencing the Pleistocene ice age. Ice and sediment cores, as well as present-day landforms, show that our current ice age probably began about thirty-five thousand years

A giant freezer in Denver, Colorado, stores ice core samples from the Greenland Ice Sheet. Carbon dioxide levels in the cores provide evidence of global warming.

ago. An abrupt temperature drop caused glaciers to begin forming on the Antarctic continent. The temperature has dropped more slowly since then. Many people consider the real beginning of our ice age to be about three million years ago. This is when temperatures became cold enough for permanent glaciers to form in the Northern Hemisphere. Right now, the earth is much colder than it has been for most of its history. The earliest humans didn't appear until about 2.5 million years ago, so humans have not experienced the earth when it was its warmest.

CHAPTER 5

REMNANTS OF AN ICE AGE

As we learned in the last chapter, the earth is halfway through its most recent interglacial period. Our planet is getting warmer, and it may continue to warm for another ten thousand years. This is a naturally occurring interglacial cycle. But most scientists think human activities, including deforestation and burning fossil fuels, are causing the planet to warm much faster than it normally would.

Whatever the cause, our climate is changing rapidly. It may be noticeably different even ten to twenty years from now. In this chapter, we will see the extent of ice cover about twenty thousand years ago, at the peak of the last ice age, and compare it with ice cover now, at the beginning of the twenty-first century.

Northern Ice Sheets

At the height of the last ice age, two major ice sheets covered most of northern North America. East of the Rocky Mountains, the 2-mile-deep (about 3.22 km) Laurentide Ice Sheet blanketed eastern Canada and the north-central and northeastern United States. West of the Rockies, the Cordilleran Ice Sheet covered western Canada and the U.S.

A space shuttle photo shows Greenland, the largest remnant of the last ice age in the Northern Hemisphere. The dark inlets around the southern coast are fiords.

Northwest. The two ice sheets met in northern Montana. They reached down to engulf regions now occupied by New York, Chicago, Seattle, and Vancouver. During this time, early humans crossed a frozen land bridge from Asia into North America.

About ten thousand years ago, the climate began to warm and the ice sheets melted, pouring their meltwater into the oceans. Sea levels rose by several hundred feet, drowning the land bridge. This stopped land migration between the continents. A channel separating Alaska from Russia, called the Bering Strait, now covers this land bridge.

Glaciers also formed in Europe and Asia. Instead of ice sheets, many smaller glaciers formed, reaching down from Scandinavia, the British Isles, and Siberia. Large glaciers formed in mountain areas, such as the Alps. In Europe, glaciers extended south, engulfing regions now containing cities like Stockholm, Berlin, and Moscow.

The Greenland Ice Sheet is the largest remnant of the last ice age in the Northern Hemisphere. Nothing lives on the ice sheet itself, but there is life on the edges of Greenland, on islands north of the Arctic Circle, and on the very northern parts of Canada, Alaska, and Siberia in Russia. This region, called the tundra, remains frozen at least ten months of the year and is too cold for trees. The only plants that can grow there are small and stunted. The tundra has a layer of permanently frozen soil called permafrost. Even in the summer, only the top few inches of soil thaws.

Antarctic Ice Sheet

Unlike the North Pole, the South Pole has a continent—Antarctica. It is surrounded by the Antarctic Ocean. On a map or globe, this ocean seems to be part of the Atlantic, Pacific, and Indian oceans. But a strong current, the Antarctic Circumpolar Current, flows in a circle around Antarctica and partly isolates it from the surrounding warmer oceans.

Antarctic glaciers formed much earlier in the present ice age than Northern Hemisphere glaciers. The most recent Antarctic ice cores go back 720,000 years, so the continent has been covered with ice at least that long.

Svalbard, a group of islands on the Arctic Circle, is the northernmost part of Norway. It still has many glaciers. These glaciers include Blomstrand Glacier on Spitsbergen Island.

Although we talk about "the Antarctic Ice Sheet," Antarctica today really has two major ice sheets. Eighty-six percent of the ice is contained in the East Antarctic Ice Sheet (EAIS). It is separated from a second, much smaller area, the West Antarctic Ice Sheet (WAIS), by the Transantarctic Mountains. The WAIS contains 11.5 percent of Antarctica's ice.

Antarctica seems far away, but its massive ice sheets impact the entire world. They directly affect climate throughout the Southern Hemisphere. Indirectly, they affect climate around the entire world. Antarctic glaciers lose ice mostly through calving of ice shelves and cliffs, rather than melting. These icebergs enter the

FRESHWATER STORED AS ICE

Exactly how much ice is there in Antarctica? If you lined up ten full glasses of water, they would represent all the freshwater on the earth. Pouring out just 1.5 glasses of water would leave 8.5 glasses. This is the amount of the earth's freshwater stored in Antarctica. Antarctica is a large continent—the size of two Australias. To hold that much ice, however, the ice sheets must be very deep. In its deepest region, the ice is almost 3 miles (4.8 km) thick. The continent's average depth is 1.33 miles (2.14 km). The weight of this much ice actually pushes the continent deeper into the ocean. Ice has buried much of the Transantarctic Mountains and other smaller mountain ranges.

Antarctic Ocean and feed the cold-water currents that eventually flow out of the Antarctic Ocean and help circulate water around the globe. Ocean circulation has a major effect on climate.

Smaller Glaciers

Large ice caps cover large parts of Iceland and the islands of Svalbard, on the Arctic Circle. Outside the Arctic, ice caps, ice fields, and mountain and valley glaciers are common at high elevations. These small glaciers are most common in southeast Alaska, the Canadian Arctic, and Canada's Yukon Territory. The Malaspina Glacier in Alaska is as big as Rhode Island.

Valley glaciers located on fiords come down to the coast and sometimes even enter the sea, forming tidewater glaciers. Tidewater glaciers are found on fiords around the world.

High mountain ranges around the world have small glaciers. Although these glaciers hold tiny amounts of ice compared to the Greenland and Antarctic ice sheets, they are more important to the everyday lives of people who live near them. In the United States, glaciers still exist in Glacier National Park in Wyoming and Rocky Mountain National Park in Colorado. In South America, many mountain glaciers and a few large ice caps cover the high reaches of the Andes.

In Europe, mountain glaciers form the basis of a large skiing and winter sports industry. Also, annual meltwater from mountain glaciers is an important water source for many regions. Important glaciers in Europe are located in the Alps of Switzerland and France and the highlands of Scotland and northern England. Another mountain range with significant amounts of glacial ice is the Himalayan Range in Asia that separates China from India and Nepal.

GLACIERS TODAY AND TOMORROW

Whether the rise in the earth's temperature is due to natural or human causes, or both, scientists are very concerned. In 2007, a group of scientists from around the world published a study collecting what is currently known about rising temperatures and how they are affecting the climate. One of their concerns is the rapid melting of glaciers, ice caps, and ice sheets. Right now, about 90 percent of the world's glaciers are shrinking.

Small Tropical Glaciers

Small mountain glaciers respond most quickly to rising temperature. This means they can serve as red flags to warn us of the possible dangers of rising temperatures. If warming continues, we can expect the melting of larger ice caps and ice sheets to increase, too.

Tropical glaciers are located fairly near the equator in Mexico, South America, and Africa. Ice still exists here in the very high mountains of these regions. Scientists at the University of Mexico predict that Mexico will lose all its glaciers within fifteen to twenty years. Heat from volcanic activity, as well as global warming, is speeding up ice melt on the Mexican volcano Popocatépetl.

Heat from its active volcano, plus rising air temperatures, are speeding up the melting of the ice cap on Mexico's Mount Popocatépetl.

In South America, glaciers occur in the Andes along the continent's west coast. Andean glaciers are disappearing rapidly, especially in Peru, which has about 70 percent of the world's tropical glaciers. Glaciers are also disappearing in Colombia, Bolivia, and Ecuador. Scientists predict that South America's glaciers could all melt within a generation. Those at lower altitudes could be gone within ten years.

More than thirty million people in South America now depend on glacial meltwater. It is particularly important for city water supplies, farming and herding, and the mining industry. Also, many people in the region depend on hydroelectric power, or energy generated by dams. Melting of glaciers will mean a need for new water and energy sources, which could cost billions of dollars.

Two of Africa's most famous mountains, Mount Kenya and Mount Kilimanjaro, are located in national parks. They are valuable tourist attractions and national symbols. Mount Kilimanjaro has been losing ice for the last century, due to local factors not related to global warming. Mount Kenya has lost ice rapidly in the past few decades. All of its permanent ice could melt within the next twenty years.

Small Temperate Glaciers

Temperate mountain glaciers in the Northern Hemisphere, and a few in the Southern Hemisphere, are found in locations having definite summer and winter seasons, such as the United States and southern Canada. Most of these glaciers are also endangered.

Lakes now fill once-glaciated valleys in the Himalayan Mountains. This is Tsho Rolpa Glacier Lake, on the border of China and Nepal.

The largest glacier area in the Southern Hemisphere, outside of Antarctica, is the Southern Ice Fields of Chile and Argentina. Like many other glaciers, the rate of ice melt has increased rapidly since the early 1990s.

The vast Himalayas in Asia are home to many of the world's highest mountains, including Mount Everest. But even these mountains are feeling the heat. In 1980, the Imjha Tse Valley in

Since 2000, more ice has melted from the Greenland Ice Sheet than has been added. Here, an iceberg calved from a coastal glacier pours meltwater into Disko Bay.

Nepal was filled with glaciers. Now, it is filled with a huge glacial lake. In the last few decades, glaciers have melted into this valley at a rate of 33 feet (10 m) per year.

People throughout the Himalayas are at great risk when glaciers melt. Already, landslides have buried villages and farms and wiped out bridges and roads. Moraines holding back glacial lakes have burst, flooding the valleys. More than two thousand of Nepal's three thousand glaciers have at least partially melted and now contain lakes. Twenty of the lakes are currently at risk of bursting and flooding the valleys below.

Melting glaciers in the European Alps are causing flooding and endangering a tourist industry that is highly dependent on skiing and snowboarding. A scientific group in Switzerland predicts that, by 2100, average summer temperatures in Europe will increase by more than 5 degrees Fahrenheit (-15 degrees Celsius), and Alpine glaciers will lose three-fourths of their ice.

And, finally, most U.S. and Canadian glaciers in the Cascades, the Rockies, and the Sierra Nevada Mountains are shrinking rapidly, too. The shrinkage is obvious in Glacier National Park, in Montana's Rocky Mountains. In the mid-1800s, this region had 150 glaciers. In 2005, all but twenty-seven had melted. Scientists estimate that, if temperatures continue to rise, they will all melt by 2030.

Both North America and Europe depend on meltwater to power hydroelectric dams. They use meltwater for water supplies and irrigation. Melting glaciers will also affect the salmon industry. Salmon swim upstream to spawn in rivers now fed by glaciers. Finally, many U.S. and Canadian glaciers are located in national parks. As in Europe, these areas will lose money when people can no longer ski or view spectacular ice-capped mountains. After all, what is Glacier National Park without its glaciers?

Melting Ice Sheets

In the 1990s, the amount of ice lost at the edges of the Greenland Ice Sheet was nearly balanced by the amount added in the center. But, in the 2000s, the mass balance shifted. Every year, the ice sheet is now losing about 20 percent more ice than it gains. The rate of ice loss doubled between 2000 and 2005. Between 2005 to 2007, Greenland ice melted at record-breaking rates.

Until recently, most scientists thought few changes were occurring in the Antarctic Ice Sheet. Because of its huge size, they thought it would not be affected much by small rises in global temperature. But, during 2002, a chunk of ice the size of Rhode Island fell off the Ross Ice Shelf and broke into icebergs. Scientists are not sure if this was due to recent climate changes, but studies show it is likely.

The most talked about impact of melting ice sheets is sea level rise. When land ice melts, it eventually flows into the oceans, increasing sea level. Melting of mountain glaciers would have almost no effect on sea level. But the two ice sheets contain 98 to 99 percent of all freshwater ice. If the Greenland Ice Sheet melted completely, it would raise world sea levels 23 feet (7 m). The Antarctic Ice Sheet would raise them 182 feet (55.47 m).

Of course, it would take thousands of years for the ice sheets to melt completely. The amount of ice currently melting from both Greenland and Antarctica, as of 2008, is raising sea level only about 0.02 inch, or half a millimeter, per year. But the problem does worry scientists. In 2007, they estimated that melting of the

POLAR BEARS IN PERIL

Polar bears live on islands and coastlines around the Arctic Circle. They migrate inland and hibernate for six to eight months of the year. When they emerge in winter, they are hungry, and what they want most to eat is the ringed seal.

To hunt their favorite food, polar bears trek miles across flat tables of sea ice in the Arctic Ocean. Hopping between ice floes, or swimming when necessary, they make their way to the open ocean where seals congregate.

But what happens to polar bears now that Arctic sea ice is melting at an alarming rate? They can no longer hop between ice floes, so they swim. Some have been spotted 60 miles (96.5 km) from shore. Although they are strong swimmers, dead ones have been found, apparently drowned in storms. Others stay on shore. They feed on the remains of whales caught by Inuit hunters—a less tasty food, and one that makes them dependent on people.

There are now only twenty thousand polar bears in the world, and their population may decrease by 30 percent in the next several decades.

Polar bears lie on ice floes and wait for seals to surface. But as ice floes melt, life in the Arctic is harder for both seals and polar bears.

Greenland Ice Sheet would raise world sea levels by only about 1 to 4 inches (25.4 to 101.6 mm) over the next century. But newer data suggest a more likely rise is 1 to 2 feet (.3 to .6 m). This would cause major problems for the millions of people currently living on islands or coasts.

A second possible impact of melting ice sheets is the release of large amounts of freshwater into the oceans. This will affect ocean currents because freshwater does not sink and ocean circulation depends on the sinking of cold, dense water off the coast of Greenland. If sinking does not occur, this disrupts circulation and could slow or stop the Gulf Stream, which brings warm water to the eastern United States and western Europe. Without this circulation, some scientists think the earth could quickly plunge into another ice age.

Ice and the Future

It is clear that our planet is getting warmer. Temperatures are increasing most rapidly near the poles, and ice is melting quickly. In temperate and tropical regions, where temperatures are already warm, even small temperature rises are melting the ice faster.

The reasons for warming temperatures and melting ice are complex. Natural climate cycles and local weather conditions play a big part. People also contribute when we drive cars, run factories, or do anything else that adds greenhouse gases to the atmosphere. At this point, no one knows for sure how much global warming is caused by each factor.

What is most important is that we recognize change is occurring and begin to adapt to it. If people understand possible dangers, such as floods or mudslides, they can prepare for them. If they know that, in the future, water supplies will be less reliable, they can develop water conservation methods and look for new water sources. And if it becomes clear to the public that humans are responsible for at least some of today's climate change, individuals and governments can look for ways to decrease the greenhouse gases that we add to the atmosphere. This will slow the planet's temperature rise and give us more time to adapt to the changing climate.

People, like all living organisms, are endlessly creative and able to adapt. Our species has lived through glacials and interglacials at least eight times before. Perhaps, in another fifty or one hundred years, there will be very little ice left on the earth. Or we may even be heading into a new ice age. Either way, we can educate ourselves, pay attention to how our climate is changing, and learn how we might be changing it. Then, we will be prepared to live happily, whatever happens to the world around us.

GLOSSARY

calve To break off a piece of an ice shelf, forming one or more icebergs.

cirque A basin at the head of a glacier formed by glacial erosion and filled with either a small glacier or a lake.

crevasse A deep crack formed in the brittle surface of a glacier.

cryosphere The frozen part of the earth's freshwater, including sea ice and glaciers.

drumlin A small hill formed by glacial deposition, having a sloping side and a steep side, and often found in groups called drumlin fields.

esker A curving ridge of sand and gravel, formed by glacial deposition.

fiord An ocean inlet that was once a glacial trough, often called a drowned river valley; also spelled fjord.

firn The stage halfway between snow and ice when a glacier is formed, consisting of compressed, rounded pellets of snow; means "old snow."

glacial (glacial period) Part of a continuing cycle during an ice age, when temperatures are lowest and glaciers are largest.

glacial till (till) Sediment that is picked up, carried, and deposited by a glacier; consists of bits of rock and soil of all sizes from clay particles to huge boulders.

glacial trough A U-shaped mountain valley formed by glacial erosion.

glacier A thick, flowing mass of ice occurring on land and made when layers of snow build up, compact, and crystallize.

greenhouse gas A type of atmospheric gas, such as carbon dioxide, that traps and circulates heat through the atmosphere, keeping the earth's temperature warm.

ice age An extremely cold period in the earth's history, when glaciers covered large parts of most continents.

ice core A cylinder of ice from an ice sheet or glacier, sometimes several miles long, obtained by drilling straight down; analysis of core layers gives information on past climates.

ice sheet A large, flat glacier that flows outward in all directions from a center where ice accumulates.

ice shelf A thick mass of ice at the edge of a glacier that extends into the ocean and floats on the water.

interglacial Part of a continuing cycle during an ice age, when temperatures warm, most or all of the ice melts, and world sea levels rise as melted land ice flows into the oceans.

mass balance The "budget" of a glacier, or the relationship between the amount of snow and ice it gains or loses.

moraine A long ridge of till pushed along and deposited by an advancing glacier as it begins to melt.

sediment core A cylinder of ocean or lake sediment, sometimes several miles long, obtained by drilling straight down.

surge The sudden, rapid movement of a glacier that has previously moved very slowly.

tarn A glacial lake formed when a glacier melts and fills a cirque.

tundra A very cold area just below the ice-covered regions of the Northern Hemisphere, which has some life but remains frozen ten months of the year.

FOR MORE INFORMATION

Canadian Cryospheric Information Network

Department of Geography and Environmental Management
University of Waterloo
200 University Avenue West
Waterloo, ON N2L 3G1
Canada
(519) 888-4567 ext. 32689
Web site: http://www.ccin.ca
This network allows access to Canadian cryospheric information.

Canadian Polar Commission

Suite 1710, Constitution Square
360 Albert Street
Ottawa, ON K1R 7X7
Canada
(888) 765-2701
Web site: http://www.polarcom.gc.ca/index.php
The Canadian Polar Commission is responsible for monitoring, promoting, and disseminating knowledge on polar regions.

NSF Office of Polar Programs (OPP)

The National Science Foundation
4201 Wilson Boulevard
Arlington, VA 2230

(703) 292-5111

Web site: http://www.nsf.gov/od/opp/about.jsp

The OPP manages and initiates NSF funding for basic research and its operational support in the Arctic and Antarctic.

Smithsonian Arctic Studies Center

P.O. Box 37012

Department of Anthropology MRC 112

Washington, DC 20013-7012

(202) 633-1887

Web site: http://www.mnh.si.edu/arctic

This center focuses on studying the cultures of the Arctic.

U.S. Antarctic Resource Center

MS 515 National Center

12201 Sunrise Valley Drive

Reston, VA 20192

(703) 648-6010

Web site: http://usarc.usgs.gov

This agency collects and shares data on the Antarctic.

Web Sites

Due to the changing nature of Internet links, Rosen Publishing has developed an online list of Web sites related to the subject of this book. This site is updated regularly. Please use this link to access the list:

http://www.rosenlinks.com/lan/glac

FOR FURTHER READING

Apte, Sunita. *Polar Regions: Surviving in Antarctica* (X-Treme Places). New York: NY: Bearport Publishing, 2005.

Carruthers, Margaret W. *Glaciers*. New York, NY: Franklin Watts, 2005.

Cherry, Lynne, and Gary Braasch. *How We Know What We Know About Our Changing Climate: Scientists and Kids Explore Global Warming* (About Our Changing Climate). Nevada City, CA: Dawn Publications, 2008.

Deem, James M. *Bodies from the Ice: Melting Glaciers and the Recovery of the Past*. Boston, MA: Houghton-Mifflin, 2008.

DK Publishing. *Arctic and Antarctic* (Eye Wonder). New York, NY: DK Children, 2006.

Gordon, John. *Glaciers* (WorldLife Library). Stillwater, MN: Voyageur Press, 2001.

Parker, Steve. *Polar Lands* (100 Things You Should Know About…). Braintree, Essex, England: Miles Kelly Publishing Ltd., 2008.

Taylor, Barbara. *Arctic & Antarctic* (Eyewitness Books). New York, NY: DK Children, 2000.

Walker, Sally M. *Glaciers* (Early Bird Earth Science). Minneapolis, MN: Lerner Publications, 2007.

Wilson, Barbara, and Vicki Leon, ed. *The Secrets of the Polar Regions: Life on Icebergs and Glaciers at the Poles and Around the World*. (Jean-Michel Cousteau Presents). Flintridge, CA: London Town Press, 2008.

BIBLIOGRAPHY

About the Great Lakes: Great Lakes Atlas. "The Glacial Era" and "The First Lakes." Retrieved November 11, 2008 (http://www.aboutthegreatlakes.com/formation.htm).

Alley, Richard B. *The Two-Mile Time Machine: Ice Cores, Abrupt Climate Change, and Our Future*. Princeton, NJ: Princeton University Press, 2000.

Anderson, Raymond R., and Jean Cutler Prior. "Glacial Boulders in Iowa." Adapted from Iowa Geology, Iowa Department of Natural Resources, November 15, 1990. Retrieved October 11, 2008 (http://www.igsb.uiowa.edu/Browse/boulders/boulders.htm).

Antarctic Connection. "Antarctic Winds & the Wind Chill Factor." Retrieved September 19, 2008 (http://www.antarcticconnection.com/antarctic/weather/wind.shtml).

Bentley, Charles R., Robert H. Thomas, and Isabella Velicogna. "Ice Sheets." 2007. United Nations Global Outlook for Ice and Snow, 6A, pp. 99–114. Retrieved August 9, 2008 (http://www.unep.org/geo/geo_ice/PDF/GEO_C6_a_LowRes.pdf).

CBS13.com. "Glaciers on Mt. Shasta Keep Growing." July 8, 2008. Retrieved November 15, 2008 (http://cbs13.com/local/mount.shasta.glaciers.2.766314.html).

CO2 Science. "West Antarctic Ice Sheet Dynamics: A Summary Review of Current Literature." 2008. Retrieved October 30, 2008 (http://scienceandpublicpolicy.org/reprint/west_antarctic_ice_sheet_dynamics.html).

Environment News Service. "Greenland Ice Sheet Rapidly
    Melting." October 20, 2006. Retrieved September 21,
    2008 (http://www.ens-newswire.com/ens/oct2006/
    2006-10-20-02.asp).

Fettes College, Edinburgh, Scotland. "Glacial Landforms in
    Central Park." Retrieved October 11, 2008 (http://www.fettes.
    com/central%20park/glacial%20erratics.htm).

Gordon, John. *Glaciers* (WorldLife Library). Stillwater, MN:
    Voyageur Press, 2001.

Hambrey, Michael, and Jurg Alean. *Glaciers*. 2nd ed. Cambridge,
    England: Cambridge University Press, 2004.

International Arctic Science Committee. "Glaciers and Ice Sheets
    in the Arctic." *Encyclopedia of Earth*, October 11, 2007.
    Retrieved August 9, 2008 (http://www.eoearth.org/article/
    Glaciers_and_ice_sheets_in_the_Arctic).

Kole, William J. "Alps Glaciers Will Melt by 2050." January 22, 2007.
    Retrieved November 15, 2008 (http://www.redorbit.com/news/
    science/810406/alps_glaciers_will_melt_by_2050/index.html#).

Macdougal, Doug. *Frozen Earth: The Once and Future Story of
    Ice Ages*. Berkeley and Los Angeles, CA: University of
    California Press, 2004.

Mayewski, Paul Andrew, and Frank White. *The Ice Chronicles: The
    Quest to Understand Global Climate Change*. Hanover, NH:
    University Press of New England, 2002.

NASA. "Antarctic Ice Loss Speeds Up, Nearly Matches Greenland
    Loss." 2008. Retrieved October 30, 2008 (http://www.nasa.
    gov/topics/earth/features/antarctica-20080123.html).

Pidwirny, Michael, Mauri Pelto, and Harold Ornes. "Glacier."
    Encyclopedia of Earth, October 19, 2006 (last revised April 24,

2008). Retrieved August 9, 2008 (http://www.eoearth.org/article/Glacier).

Roach, John. "Greenland's Ice Melt Grew by 250 Percent, Satellites Show." National Geographic News, September 20, 2006. Retrieved September 21, 2008 (http://news.nationalgeographic.com/new/2006/09/060920-greenland-ice.html).

Select Committee on Energy Independence and Global Warming. "Melting Arctic Circle Ice Drives Polar Bears Closer to Extinction." Retrieved November 24, 2007 (http://global-warming.house.gov/impactzones/arctic).

Selters, Andy. *Glacier Travel & Crevasse Rescue*. Rev. ed. Seattle, WA: The Mountaineers Books, 2006

Solomon, Susan, Dahe Qin, et al., eds. *Climate Change 2007: The Physical Science Basis. Working Group I Contribution to the Fourth Assessment Report of the Intergovernmental Panel on Climate Change*. Cambridge, England, and New York, NY: Cambridge University Press, 2007.

Tarbuck, Edward J., and Frederick K. Lutgens. *Earth Science*. 10th ed. Upper Saddle River, NJ: Prentice Hall, Pearson Education, Inc., 2003.

U.S. Department of the Interior. "Age of the Earth." U.S. Geological Survey, 2007. Retrieved November 3, 2008 (http://pubs.usgs.gov/gip/geotime/age.html).

INDEX

A

abrasion, 22
Antarctic Ice Sheet, 9, 15–16, 41–43, 44, 50
arêtes, 26
avalanches, 8, 12, 15, 23

B

basal sliding, 18, 19
Bering Glacier, 18
boulder trains, 29

C

calving, 15, 42
cirques, 25–26
Cordilleran Ice Sheet, 39
crevasses, 8, 18, 19
cryosphere, 6

D

drainage basins, 21
drumlins, 28

E

eskers, 28, 29

F

fiords, 25, 43
firn, 12, 15

G

glacial
  advance and retreat, 13–17, 28
  deposition, 26, 28–29, 31
  erosion, 22–26
  erratics, 29, 32
  formation, 7, 10–12, 38, 41
  lakes, 25–26, 28–29, 31, 32, 49
  movement, downhill, 13, 17–19, 21, 28
  surges, 18
  till, 19, 21, 26, 28, 29, 31
  troughs, 25, 26
glacials vs. interglacials, 36, 53
Glacier National Park, 44, 49, 50
glaciers, rising temperatures and, 12, 15, 16, 39, 45–47, 49–53
glaciers, types of
  alpine, 9
  continental, 9, 36
  mountain, 9, 11, 12, 14, 15, 17, 43, 44, 45, 50
  temperate, 47, 49–50
  tidewater, 43
  tropical, 45–46
  valley, 23, 28, 43

global warming, 45, 47, 52
Great Lakes, 4, 31
greenhouse gases, 35, 53
Greenland Ice Sheet, 9, 16–17, 41, 44, 50, 52

H

hanging valleys, 25
hydroelectric power, 46, 49
hydrologic cycles, 6

I

ice
  caps, 9, 43, 44, 45
  cores, 35
  fields, 4, 9, 43, 47
  shelves, 9, 21, 42
  streams, 21
ice ages, documenting, 33–38
icebergs, 6, 9, 12, 15, 42, 50
interglacial cycles, 36, 39, 53

K

kettles, 29, 31

L

landslides, 49
Laurentide Ice Sheet, 39

M

Malaspina Glacier, 43
mass balance, 13, 50
moats, 8
moraines, 26, 28, 30, 32, 49

movement over till, 18, 19, 21
mudslides, 53

N

North Pole, 4, 6, 9, 32, 36, 41

O

ogives, 21
outwash plains, 29

P

permafrost, 41
plastic deformation, 18–19
plucking, 22
polar bears, 51
polar deserts, 11

R

rockslides, 23
Ross Ice Shelf, 9, 50

S

sea ice, 6, 51
South Pole, 4, 6, 9, 41
Southern Ice Fields, 47

T

tarns, 25–26
tundra, 41

W

water cycles, 6
Wisconsin Glacier, 31

Y

Yosemite Valley, 4, 25

Z

zone of fracture, 19

About the Author

Carol Hand has a Ph.D. in zoology with a concentration in ecology/environmental science. She has taught college and written for standardized testing companies. For the past ten years, she has worked for a nationally known education company, writing middle and high school curricula in environmental, earth, and life sciences.

Photo Credits

Cover, pp. 4–5, 23, 24–25 Wikimedia Commons; p. 7 © Momatiuk-Eastcott/Corbis; p. 8 © www.istockphoto.com/lorenzo puricelli; pp. 10–11 © Kennan Ward/Corbis; p. 14 Arctic-Images/Getty Images; pp. 16–17 © Gerry Bishop/Visuals Unlimited; p. 20 © Beth Davidow/Visuals Unlimited; p. 27 © Dr. Marli Miller/Visuals Unlimited; p. 30 © www.istockphoto.com/eva serrabassa; p. 33 © Alinari Archives/Corbis; p. 34 © AP Images; p. 38 © Roger Ressmeyer/Corbis; p. 40 NASA; p. 42 © Robert Harding World Imagery/Corbis; p. 46 © www.istockphoto.com/Marco Regalia; p. 47 © Macduff Everton/Corbis; p. 48 © Paul Souders/Corbis; p. 51 © www.istockphoto.com/Jan Will.

Designer: Les Kanturek; Editor: Bethany Bryan
Photo Researcher: Amy Feinberg